TravelMates

HOME 1000 M.
BEACH 30 M.

TravelMates

Fun Games Kids Can Play in the Car or on the Go—No Materials Needed

Story Evans and Lise O'Haire

Three Rivers Press, New York

Copyright © 1997 by Story Evans and Lise O'Haire

Published by Three Rivers Press, a division of Crown Publishers, Inc., 201 East 50th Street, New York, New York 10022. Member of the Crown Publishing Group.

Random House, Inc. New York, Toronto, London, Sydney, Auckland
www.randomhouse.com

THREE RIVERS PRESS and colophon are trademarks of Crown Publishers, Inc.

Printed in the United States of America

Design and illustration by Jennifer Harper

Library of Congress Cataloging-in-Publication Data is available upon request.

ISBN 0-517-88760-6

10 9 8 7 6 5 4

To our children, McCrea, Madeleine, Chelsea, Maggie, Abby, Mandi, Megan, and Drew,
who give us great joy and inspiration.
To our husbands, Michael and Tony, who encourage our dreams.
To our parents, Judy and Carl and Connie and John, with love and gratitude.

Author's Note

This collection of classic children's travel games was developed from numerous sources. Many were invented or reinvented by the authors and their children and friends. The origins of many of the games are lost in the mists of time and they are now known by different titles and descriptions. Variations may be found in almost every country and culture in the world, and through the ages these games have contributed much pleasure to all.

Contents

Introduction
"Ready, Set, Go"

Are your children bored while traveling in a car, train, plane, bus, or waiting in a restaurant or a doctor's office? They don't have to be. Imagination, memory, and mind are the only things needed in order to play these classic children's games. These games can be played between children or between adults and children. They will be almost as much fun as reaching your destination or having your dinner arrive, and they are invaluable for providing hours of fun for all ages and varieties of travelers. The possibilities are limited only by your creativity. Let's play!

Making a pleasant experience out of traveling with children on a vacation or holiday visit to grandparents, or waiting at the doctor's office or for a meal to arrive, rests mainly on one thing: keeping children occupied during the hours they're confined to the car, train, plane, bus, table, or waiting room. Adults generally have little trouble filling their time in these small environments, but most children won't spend more than a few minutes with a magazine or book. The passing scenery quickly bores

them, and the stimulation and fear of strange places, unfamiliar situations, and new events can create anything but a calm, enjoyable trip or wait.

TravelMates came into being because a couple of well-traveled-with-children parents wanted to find an answer to "How are we going to keep them occupied with something creative, entertaining, and portable?" This collection of children's games is invaluable for any trip or transport. Playing the games requires only the players and their imaginations, memories, minds, and humor. You'll play them again and again and in more than one way. They have been field-tested by the most demanding and critical users they will ever have, their creators.

For easy access to age-appropriate games, six categories have been designed:

- **Two to Three Years Old:** Fun for Ages Two to Ninety-Nine
  These are your most elementary games, but enjoyed by all.
- **Four Years Old:** I'm Four and I Can Play
  Hey, you know four-year-olds, they can do it NOW!
- **Kindergarten:** If You Show Me How, I Can Do It, Too
  Most can't read yet, but if one explains how to, they have a good grasp of details.

- **First and Second Grade:** Reader Ready

  These children are at various stages of reading, and they have started learning addition and subtraction.

- **Third and Fourth Grade:** Think and Do It for Fun

  Solid readers, these children are problem-solving now and having fun with it.

- **Fifth and Sixth Grade:** Challenge Me Now

  Skilled at advanced reasoning, these children have a broad knowledge of people, places, and things.

Two to Three Years Old:
Fun for Ages Two to Ninety-Nine

Statues

Want some action? Play this game. Choose one player to be the caller. Everybody moves around in their seat. The caller says "Freeze" and all the players become statues. The one to remain frozen for the longest time is the winner. The winner is the caller for the next round.

You can also play this game by asking everyone to make crazy faces and movements. When the caller says "Freeze," the caller decides who is the strangest statue, or the funniest or the ugliest or whatever description she chooses.

Sightseeing

What kind of sights might you see while you are traveling? If you are traveling in the country, you might pass by farms with cows, pigs, and horses. If you are on a train, you might pass through a town with different buildings and water towers alongside the tracks. If you are on an airplane, you might see all different shapes of clouds outside the windows or a variety of outfits on the people going up and down the aisles.

Play this game with two players, or play it with everyone divided into two teams, one team taking

the left-hand side of your car, train, plane, or restaurant and the other team the right side. Choose one thing you are all going to look for, such as men with striped shirts, buildings, or cows, for example. The first team to spot ten of the chosen thing wins.

To make this game a little more challenging, choose your object as before but narrow it down—for example, men with striped shirts and black hair, buildings with satellite dishes, or black-and-white-spotted cows.

Sweet and Sour

Who's sweet and who's sour? As you travel in a bus, car, or train, wave to the people you pass by. If they wave back, they are sweet; if they don't, they're sour. What did you find out?

Curiously Quiet

This will be a nice break for Mom, Dad, or whoever is leading this trip. How long can everyone be quiet? Choose someone to be the timer. The timer will announce "Go," at which point everyone will be quiet. The object of this game is to see who can be quiet for the longest time. If a player needs a break, he can signal to the timer for a time-out. Everyone can stop being quiet, but when the timer says "Go" again, you have to be quiet. The player who is quiet for the longest period of time is the winner, but as each person goes out, the timer can tell them how long they were quiet. The announcer can also pick an object (for example, a yellow house, a barn, a man with a hat, etc.) and the players remain quiet until they see the chosen object.

Runaway Raindrops

Great for a rainy-day trip. Each player looks out his window and chooses a raindrop at the top of the window. At the count of three, all players say, "READY, SET, GO." Each player watches his raindrop travel down the window. When it reaches the bottom, he says, "Finished." The first player whose raindrop reaches the bottom is the winner. Remember, one raindrop often merges with another one, making a larger raindrop, but it is still yours. More than one player can use a window; there just has to be enough space between your raindrops.

You can also try to imagine what the runaway raindrops look like: an octopus, an ice-cream sundae, a flower? Have everyone describe what has happened to their raindrop.

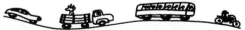

Wrap It Up

Traveling is usually an adventure with lots of new and fun experiences. Take some time to think about your trip and have each player name five things he enjoyed. It's a wonderful way to wrap up the day or your journey by remembering the trip's highlights.

Anticipation

The anticipation of a trip is always exciting. As you start your trip or as you begin each day, have each player tell the others what she is looking forward to. For example, "I'm looking forward to the boat ride" or "seeing Aunt Jane" or "going to the museum" or "seashell collecting on the beach." It's always fun to find out what everyone is looking forward to.

Changing Clouds

Look up in the sky and see all the wonderful clouds. Clouds come in all sizes and shapes and are constantly changing. What do you think they look like? Pick a cloud and tell everyone what you think it could be. Is it a magic genie, a cat, a circle, or a constellation?

You can also try playing this game by imagining that the sky is a zoo, a cartoon, a farm, or anything you want. How many animals or cartoon figures can you see?

Four Years Old:
I'm Four and I Can Play

Shake, Rattle, and Roll

Music is the game; tap it, hum it, what's the name? The object of this game is to hum or clap out a tune and have the other players guess what it is. Choose one player to start. She will decide whether she's going to hum or clap out the tune. For example, it might be "Twinkle, Twinkle, Little Star." The first player to correctly identify the tune as "Twinkle, Twinkle, Little Star" would be the next player to select a tune. If no one guesses the tune, the first player announces the tune and then goes on to another one.

Holidays and Hopefuls

Everybody has customs and traditions they associate with different holidays. Halloween might bring memories of pumpkins or haunted houses, Thanksgiving might be remembered with turkeys and things that people are thankful for, and St. Patrick's Day might bring to mind four-leaf clovers. Choose a holiday and have everyone talk about what they remember about that holiday, what they do then, and what is special about it.

Christmas, Valentine's Day, St. Patrick's Day, Easter, Memorial Day, Fourth of July, Labor Day,

and Hanukkah are just some to start you off. Create your own holiday with its own traditions, such as St. Boodlebug's Day. On that day, each person in the family might give another person in the family an unsigned card that tells them why they are special. Each person guesses who their card is from. When you play Holidays and Hopefuls, you can share your memories of this special holiday in your family.

These Are a Few of My Favorite Things

Everyone gets a turn and it's fun to hear about everyone's favorite things. Choose one player to start, who begins by choosing a question such as "What is your favorite food?" Everyone answers. For example, "My favorite food is macaroni and cheese" or "corn on the cob" or "ice-cream sundaes" or "chicken fingers." When that round has finished, select another player to ask what everyone's favorite something is, such as movie, yogurt, book, or game. You might be surprised by what you find out.

For a twist, ask other players to guess what your favorite thing is. For example, you might ask the other players to guess your favorite dessert, color, activity, or teacher.

Colors, Colors, Colors

Colors are often associated with things—for example, yellow with the sun, green with grass, white with snow, pink with Easter, or black with a spider. Choose one player to start. That player chooses a color, and each player in turn says something that

he associates with that color. For example, with blue, it may be blueberries, ink, berry punch, the ocean, boysenberry jam, the sky, or jeans. When you have exhausted the possibilities, choose a new color and start another round.

Catching Colors

Blue Explorer, red Chevy Lumina, white Voyager. How many car colors can you catch? Each person selects a color. No two players can choose the same color. The first person to spot ten different cars of his color wins.

For another variation, which is especially fun on winding roads, you might have each player try to guess what color the next car coming around the bend will be. For each correct guess, you receive one point. The first to reach ten wins.

Yet another version is to catch two- or four-door cars as they whiz by. Decide which you are going after. The first player to spot twenty wins.

Thumping Thumbs

It's fun, it's silly, it's thumping thumbs. It takes two people, or you can have pairs of players if there are more of you traveling. Two players lock right hands with all the fingers except the thumb. The thumb remains out. Once the two hands are locked, the players say, "One, two,

three, I declare thumb war."

On each count, move the thumb. Beginning on one, move left to right; on two, right to left; on three, left to right; and so on as you say the rest of the phrase. Play then begins. The object is to see whether you can pin the other player's thumb down with your thumb. You can't open the locked hands or move them around. This is good for burning up some of that pent-up energy.

I Spy

A classic detective game. Choose one player to start. Look around and decide on an object that all the players can see. Begin by saying, "I spy something . . ." (describe what you see). For example, you could say "green" or "round" to give the other players a clue. The other players ask questions to figure out what you spy, and you can only answer their questions with a yes or no. The player who guesses correctly takes over as the spy.

For a change of pace, try playing this game by announcing that you spy something that begins with a letter, such as S, for steering wheel.

Sounding Fun

As you travel, you will see and hear many things. If you are in a car, it might be a truck passing by, boats sailing on the water below a bridge, or a motorcycle zooming past. If you are on a train, you might be going through a tunnel, riding past cows on a farm, or passing another train. If you are on an airplane, you might see clouds outside the window, the captain or a flight attendant, or a flashing seat-belt sign.

Use your imagination and make up sounds for each of the sights you see. Some sights have sounds everyone knows—*moo moo* for a cow, or *vrrroom* for a motorcycle, for example. Others don't. If a cloud could make a noise, what would it be? Could it be *wheee*? An airplane captain could be *eye-eye,* or a flashing seat-belt sign *blink blink.* Agree on the sounds you will make for each sight and let the play begin. This can be a bit noisy if you spot three or four things at once and everyone is making different sounds, but it will certainly be fun.

Safety Alert

Join the safety patrol and see what you can spot. It's not safe not to wear a seat belt, or to walk across the street against a red light, or to go through a stop sign, or to Rollerblade without a helmet or knee, elbow, or wrist pads, or to ride a bicycle without a helmet. Players are on the alert for unsafe actions. Each unsafe action sighted earns a high five for the player who spots it.

Now join the litter patrol. See how many litterbugs you spot. Do you see people thowing trash out of car windows or dropping candy or gum wrappers on the street? A high five to each player who spots a litterbug.

Neon Brights

It's flashy, it's bright, it's neon! Choose a color—red, blue, white, green, pink, yellow, or orange. No two players can choose the same color. The first player to spot five different neon signs of her color wins. For example, if you see a pink neon sign that says MCCREA'S RIBS, and your color is

pink, you have the first of the five neon signs you need to spot in your color.

You can also play this game by having each player guess what color the next neon sign you pass will be.

Lions and Tigers and Bears . . . Oh My!

Lions and tigers and bears, oh my! Sometimes when you are traveling you will see all different kinds of animals along the way. If you're driving by farms, it might be cows, sheep, or horses. Touring in Africa, you might see gazelles, giraffes, or elephants. Hiking in the woods, you might come upon rabbits, squirrels, or deer. In this game players count the different animals they see while traveling. The first player to sight ten different kinds of animals wins the game.

To make the game a little bit different, you might choose one type of animal and establish how many of this animal a player has to see in order to win.

Simon Says

Feeling restless? Need to release some stored-up energy? It's time for Simon Says. Choose one player to be Simon. Simon tells the other players what to do by first saying "Simon says." For example, "Simon says clap your hands." The other players must do what Simon says. However, if the first player were to say "Clap your hands" and not "Simon says clap your hands" and you clapped your hands, you would be out because Simon fooled you and didn't tell you *he* was saying to do

it. Continue the game until there is one player left. That person is the next Simon. Remember you are sitting, so think of things you can do while sitting, like touching your nose or ear, sticking out your tongue, pointing to something, or pretending to cough or wink.

Mother, May I?

Say "Mother, may I?" and you are in the game. Forget and you are out of the game. Choose one player to be "Mother." Mother tells the other players what to do—for example, pretend to sneeze. The other players must do what Mother says, but before they do they must say, "Mother, may I?" A player is out if she forgets to ask, "Mother, may I?" Continue the game until there is one player left. That person is the next Mother. Remember to think of things players can do while sitting.

The Name Game

Think of how all your names sound. How many words can you rhyme with each person's name? For example, Abby rhymes with cabbie, flabby, gabby, and Matt rhymes with cat, sat, pat, bat. Some names are easy, some names are hard. The player who rhymes the most words with each name is the winner.

Animal Talk

Great for pretending! Each player thinks of an animal and asks the others playing if they were that animal how would they talk. For example, "If you were a cat, how would you talk?" Continue with as many animals as everyone can think up. You also might want to add gestures to characterize the animal talking.

Another way to play this game is to choose one player and have that player think of an animal and whisper what it is to another player. Talk like the animal that has been whispered to you and see who can guess the animal correctly. The player who guesses correctly decides on the next animal and whispers it to someone else.

Pat Your Head, Rub Your Stomach

Harder than it sounds! See if each player can pat her head and rub her stomach in a circular motion at the same time. Try reversing it, patting your stomach and rubbing your head in a circular motion. Can you do this while singing a song, or reciting the alphabet, or telling a story? You can make up other activities like this with two

motions that are hard to do—for example, blinking your eyes and sticking your tongue out or snapping your fingers and moving your head side to side while reciting the alphabet backward. The crazier, the better!

Fabulous Food

Chocolate: uummmm, good. Each player thinks up a way to describe food—tart, horrible, sweet, refreshing, or delicious. Players, in turn, name foods that fit that description. For example, "horrible" might be unsweetened chocolate, brussels sprouts, rotten bananas, mayonnaise, or any other food someone thinks is terrible. Continue until you cannot think of any more. Then start a new food description with the second player and continue until everyone's had a turn.

Backseat Hide-and-Seek

Sitting-still hide-and-seek? It's possible and it's fun! Choose a player to start. Pretend that you have hidden yourself somewhere well known to everyone playing, such as your house, neighborhood, a store, school, playground, grandmother's house, or anywhere else. The one who is pretending to be hiding chooses a spot in the place. The other players ask questions to figure out the hiding place, which can only be answered with a yes or no. The player who discovers the hiding place is the next one to hide.

Double your fun by guessing the place first and the hiding spot second. For example, a player might choose a place, the circus, and the hiding spot, the tiger's cage.

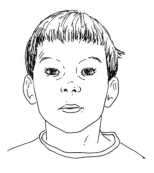

Excellent Expressions

Put on your poker face. Think of all the emotions you can act out, such as sad, happy, angry, worried, sleepy, or scared. Each player thinks of one and everyone in turn acts it out using a facial expression. Or have one person act out an expression and have the other players try and guess what it is. Who's the best actor or actress? Who made you laugh the most?

Kindergarten: If You Show Me How, I Can Do It, Too

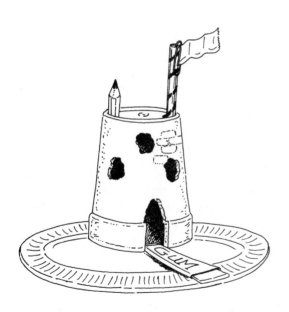

Imagination Station

A gold chain bracelet is usually thought of simply as a pretty piece of jewelry worn on one's wrist. But if you used your imagination, you could think of it as a rope to be thrown up a mountain to rescue a unicorn stuck on a ledge. Each of you thinks of an object and asks the other players to imagine what else it might be. For example, a straight pin might be a walking stick for a cricket, a dollar bill could be a blanket for the tooth fairy, or a pencil could be a baton.

Perfectly Powerful Pantomimes

A pantomime is silent acting. You can't say anything, but you can use your arms, legs, face, or any part of your body to act out something. For example, you might pantomime brushing your teeth by pretending to get the toothpaste, unscrew the cap, put some toothpaste on your toothbrush, and then brush your teeth.

The first player chooses something to pantomime. The player to correctly guess what he is acting out does the next pantomime. Another way to play the game is by having a selected player tell the other players what to pantomime, so that every player acts out the same pantomime. After the game is over, the selected player chooses another player to begin the next round.

Things to pantomime might include nursery rhymes, planting seeds in a garden, blowing out birthday candles, or talking on the telephone. You can also break this game into categories, such as animals, food, clothes, or occupations.

Stop, Look, and Listen

How much do you remember? How much can you hear? Choose one player to be the timer. When that player says "Go," look hard, look everywhere for one minute. When the timer says "Stop," players close their eyes and recount everything they saw. It's fun to hear about what everyone notices.

Another way to play this game is to have everyone shut their eyes for one minute. At the end of a minute, each player takes turns recounting everything he heard.

Palm Reading

Use your senses. It is time to guess letters written on your palm and figure out what word they spell. The first player thinks of a word and then asks another player to close her eyes and hold out the palm of her hand. The first player traces the first letter of the word onto the second player's palm. The second player tries to guess the letter. When she has guessed the letter correctly, she closes her palm to erase the letter. Still keeping her eyes shut, she opens her palm again. Now she is ready for the next letter. Play continues until she gets the word. Take turns playing it with each player. Pairs of players can play at the same time.

If you have the space and it's not dangerous to turn your back to another player, try having the letters traced on your back. The first player traces a whole word on the second player's back and the second player has to guess what it is. You may have to trace it a second time and set a time limit for guessing. It's easier to start with short words first.

Tongue Twisters

Feeling silly? Play this game and do it in rounds. One of you starts by thinking of a tongue twister. Some old favorites are "Peter Piper picked a peck of pickled peppers," "Rubber baby buggy bumper," "How much wood could a woodchuck chuck if a woodchuck could chuck wood?" and "Sally sells seashells by the seashore." See how many times each of you can say one of these tongue twisters (or another one you make up)

before you twist the words. The player who can say the phrase the most times correctly and quickly wins that round. Now try another one.

Got this down pat? Try making up your own phrase with each word starting with the same letter. Using G, for example, "Gorgeous George gorged gallons of gourds gallantly." Hear the laughter or the praise.

Animals, Animals, Animals

Animals everywhere. Each player secretly decides on an animal he wants to be. Choose one player to start. Tell the other player two facts about your animal, such as "I have whiskers and fur," but do not name the animal. Now see who can guess correctly what animal you are. The person who guesses correctly is the next to choose an animal.

Seeing and Remembering

How much of what you see can you remember? Select one person to collect ten items around you, such as a penny, a watch, a pen, a candy wrapper, a mint, keys, a brush, a bottle cap, a pretzel, and a pair of glasses—anything that's handy. Display them on a solid surface—an airplane tray, the seat of a car, a magazine, the top of a cooler—for one minute, then cover them up. How many items can you remember?

For variety, choose a player to start a sentence using something she sees—for example, "There's a field of flowers." The second player repeats the first player's sentence and adds to the sentence using something that he sees—for example, "There's a field of flowers and a spotted dog." Each player, in turn, repeats the entire sentence

Letters Everywhere

Letters are everywhere—on billboards, trains, rooftops, barns, taxicabs, trucks, road signs, and buildings. The object of this game is to find all the letters of the alphabet in order from A to Z, using the letters that you see while traveling. The first player begins with the letter A and announces the word or phrase she sees beginning with A—for example, a road sign saying ATLANTA 150 MILES. Player two continues with the letter B, found, for instance, on the sign BP GAS NEXT EXIT. In passing a billboard, you might see MADELEINE'S GARDENS, which could be the letter M or G. Each player, in turn, continues through the alphabet. You lose your turn if you cannot find a sight beginning with your letter.

You can also play this game by finding all the let-

and adds on a new part using something he sees. If you cannot remember the sentence or add to it, you are out.

ters of the alphabet in order, from A to Z, using the sights you see. A might be found when an automobile passes by, B when you see a barbecue restaurant, C when a cat is spotted along the road, and so on. Players cannot use the same object. The first player to complete the alphabet wins the game.

Rhymin' Timin'

Many words rhyme with each other. In this game you are asking other players to discover the word you are thinking of by giving rhyming clues. The first player thinks of a secret word and gives a clue as to what the word is by thinking of a word that rhymes with it. For example, "I'm thinking of something you sleep on that rhymes with red" (bed), or "I'm thinking of something you play with that rhymes with cat" (bat), or "I'm thinking of something you might take a trip on that rhymes with rain" (train). The first player to guess the word is the next to rhyme-time a word.

Me, Myself, and I

How do you see yourself? What would you say about yourself? What would others say about you? Think of four words to describe yourself—for example, "six," "funny," "nice," "athletic." Each player, in turn, adds a word to describe you. Continue until players run out of words to describe you, then choose another player for everyone to describe.

To test your memory, have each player repeat the first four words about the player and then their own descriptive word. Each player, in turn, repeats the previous words and then adds their own. Play continues until only one person can remember everything that describes the person.

Rock, Scissors, Paper

Rock, scissors, paper—which one will come up first? This is a sign-language game for two or more people. Use these signs for rock, scissors, paper:

Rock: Make a fist.

Scissors: Hold out your index and middle fingers to make a V, keeping the other fingers down.

Paper: Hold your hand flat, palm down.

The rules for this game are:

- Rock wins over scissors because rock can break scissors.
- Scissors wins over paper because scissors can cut paper.
- Paper wins over rock because paper can cover a rock.

To play, each player puts both hands behind his back and secretly chooses a sign. Players count to three and then put out their right hand, making the sign they have chosen. Players receive one point for each win. See who is the winner after five rounds. If all players put out the same sign, it is a tie and they must do it over again to determine a winner.

Down by the Banks

This is a musical clapping game for two people using a musical rhyme, "Down by the Banks."

Down by the banks of the hanky panks
Where the bullfrogs jump from bank to bank,
Singing: eeps, eips, oops, ohps,
Chilly, willy, ding, dong!

In rhythm begin:

On first line:

Clap both hands to thighs, clap both hands together, clap right hand to TravelMate,
clap both hands to thighs, clap both hands together, clap both hands to TravelMate three times.

On second line:

Clap both hands to thighs, clap both hands together, clap left hand to TravelMate,
clap both hands to thighs, clap both hands together, clap both hands to TravelMate three times.

On third line:

Clap both hands to thighs, clap both hands together, clap right hand to TravelMate, clap both hands to thighs, clap both hands together.

On fourth line:

Clap both hands to thighs, clap both hands together, clap left hand to TravelMate, clap both hands to thighs.

Clap your hands, saying a word or two of the rhyme for each movement. Some of the words need to be said over two movements. See how fast you can do it. Can you adapt this to another rhyme, poem, or song you know? How about the classic, "A Sailor Went to Sea," or "Peter Pumpkin Eater"? Change the clapping movements to fit, or create your own.

You Can't Say That

You can't say that! Have you ever tried not to say a word that is so natural to you, such as "no," "we," "the," "going," "maybe," "please," "or," "to," or "can," for example? Choose a word and set a time limit of ten minutes. Begin talking. Each time you say the word by mistake and are caught, it's a point against you. The player with the fewest points at the end wins. The winner can choose the next word you can't say. The game might go like this:

Player one:	"Let's choose 'I' as the word we can't say. Do you want to go to the park today?"
Player two:	"No, don't want to go. What else do you want to do?"
Player three:	"Play baseball."
Player one:	"Want to play, but I forgot my glove."
Player two:	"You have a point against you, you said 'I'."

Instead of points against you, you can choose to tickle the player who says the word you can't say. It is guaranteed to make you laugh, but don't include the driver in this version.

Stop, Look, and Guess

Red, yellow, green—how many traffic lights will you see? What's your guess? The object of this game is to estimate the number of traffic lights the car will drive through without stopping. Each player guesses a number. The person who guesses the correct number or else is closest to the correct number wins.

You can also play this game by having each player guess the number of stop signs, potholes, or speed bumps the car will come to or go over before it goes a mile, gets to the next town, arrives at your friend's house, or reaches whatever other destination you choose. The person who guesses correctly or is closest to the correct number wins.

Only Opposites

Opposites are endless. The object of this game is to choose a word and challenge your TravelMates to say its opposite, such as freezing and boiling. Let everyone have a turn. Mean and nice, happy and sad, and black and white are other examples.

I Packed My Grandmother's Trunk

This game will test your memory. You are on a trip and so is Grandmother. The first player begins with "I packed my Grandmother's trunk and in it I put (choose anything you want)"—a dress, for example. The next player repeats, "I packed my grandmother's trunk and in it I put a dress and (now add something else)"—an elephant or a glass of milk, for example. Each player, in turn, will repeat the sentence and add something new. If you cannot remember what is already in the trunk, you are out. Play continues until only one person can remember everything that has been added to Grandmother's trunk.

Words, Words, Words

Words, words, words. Every word makes you think of another one. The object of this game is to name a word associated with the one the previous player says. The first player, for example, might say "sweater." The second player might say "cold." Now the second player says a new word, such as "beach." The third player has to come up with an associated word, such as "sand." Play continues from player to player with each naming a new word associated with the previous player's word and then naming a new word for the next player.

You can also play this game by having each player name a word association for what the previous player came up with, creating a word chain. For example:

Player one:	sweater
Player two:	cold
Player three:	snow
Player one:	mitten

The word chain could continue—"finger," "hand," "wave," "good-bye," and so on—until you run out of words. Then start out again with a new word.

Round and Round the Story Goes

Use your imagination and creativity to compose a story. Choose one person to start. That person will begin the story by setting up the situation and the characters. Stop after a few sentences or even midsentence and turn the story over to another player by saying "And then . . ." Each player adds on to the story until the last player draws the story to an end.

Another way you can play this game is by continuing on in rounds and thereby making the story longer. You can also design the story so that each player ends her turn by leaving the character in a situation from which the next player has to save him. Or you can decide from the start on a particular type of story, such as adventure, mystery, science fiction, fairy tale, or comedy.

What Am I Eating?

Can you guess what I'm eating? The purpose of this game is to try to figure out what kind of food another player is eating. Choose one player to start. That player selects a food and begins the game by saying "I'm eating . . ." The other players, in turn, will ask questions to guess what food it is. The questions players can ask are limited to taste, color, texture, smell, whether it is generally eaten cooked or raw, and whether it is eaten at breakfast, lunch, dinner, or as a snack. Their questions can only be answered with a yes or no. The person who guesses correctly is the next to select a food. You might want to set a time limit of between five and ten minutes for the game. Here's how a game might go:

Player one:	"I'm eating . . ."	Player two:	"Is it red?"
Player one:	"No."	Player three:	"Is it a breakfast food?"
Player one:	"Yes."	Player two:	"Is it sweet?"
Player one:	"Yes."	Player three:	"Do you eat it raw?"
Player one:	"Yes."	Player two:	"Is it a cereal?"
Player one:	"No."	Player three:	"Is it blueberries?"
Player one:	"Yes."		

One Potato, Two Potato . . .

Use your hands, not your brains, for this one. This is a hand game for two or more people. It works best when everyone can put their hands together in front of them, using their fists to form a circle. Adapt it to fit your travel space. Have each player shape both hands into a fist and put them in front of him. The first player, called the Potato Masher, puts his left fist into the circle. The Potato Masher begins the chant:

One potato, two potato, three potato, four, five potato, six potato, seven potato, more.

As the rhyme is chanted, the Potato Masher taps the fists of the other players with his right hand, starting with his own left hand and moving around the circle clockwise. When the Potato

Masher comes to what would be his right hand, he hits his chin instead of the right hand he is using to tap the other players' fists. If a player's

fist is tapped on the word "more," that player puts her fist behind her back. Continue with the next fist in line and play until only one fist is left. The person whose fist that is becomes the next Potato Masher and starts the next round.

Secret Signs

Develop a secret code. Choose signs to identify words, such as making a small O with your thumb and forefinger, or holding just your forefinger and middle finger up and bending them at the knuckles, or winking, or rubbing your fingers, or patting your stomach, etc.—any expression that can be seen but does not make a noise. You can play this game several ways.

One, you can design a secret and special code, which no one else will understand, between yourself and one or both of your parents, friends, or brother or sister.

Two, you can have every player choose a sign to identify himself. Begin the game by performing your own sign and then everyone else's. Each player, in turn, will repeat everyone's sign. If you cannot, you are out. See how fast you can go. Play continues until one person is left.

Three, you can perform your sign and then someone else's. That person then does her own sign and then someone else's. If you do not respond quickly, or give a sign of someone out of the game, you are out. See how far you can go. Play until there is only one person left.

Punchbuggie

Who would have thought that a Volkswagen Beetle would have become so famous? This small car is widely recognized and has a large following. To play this game, you need to spot a Volkswagen Beetle—let's say a red one. The player who sees one first would cry out, "Punchbuggie red, no punchbacks, I say, I said it first," lightly punching anybody close to him (except the driver, of course). "No punchbacks" means that you cannot punch back the person who punched you. This game can go on and on as everyone scans for Punchbuggies throughout their travels.

This game would also be fun if you wanted to choose a different kind of car and make up a saying for it if you spot it. See what you can invent!

First and Second Grade: Reader Ready

Anteater Alphabet Nonsense

What did the anteater do? The object of this game is to go through the alphabet describing nonsensically what the Anteater does. The first player starts by saying "A is for Anteater." Each player, in turn, makes up something with one word about what happens to the Anteater, with the appropriate letter. For example:

"**A** is for Anteater."   "**B** bit it."   "**C** caught it."

"**D** devoured it."   "**E** enjoyed it."   "**F** flaunted it."

"**G** gets it."   "**H** handled it."   "**I** invited it."

"**J** jumped it," and so on through the alphabet.

A player who cannot think of something with his letter is out. (X, Y, and Z might be a problem, so leave them out of the game if they make it too difficult.)

Laugh Attack

How long can you last before a laugh attack? Choose one player to start who will be "It," then come up with a silly phrase—for example, "Goobly Globbly Blinky Goblins" or "Inky Pinky Ponkey Doodle Donkey"—which will be used by "It" to answer questions. Each time other players ask "It" a question, "It" must answer with the chosen phrase without laughing. For example, a player might ask "It" "What did you do today?" or "Who are you going to see?" If "It" answers, "Goobly Globbly Blinky Goblins" and laughs, she is out. Give every player a chance to be "It." The player who answers the most questions without laughing is the winner.

What Would You Do If . . .

You've just won the lottery. How would you spend the money? Everyone thinks up a "What would you do if" question and asks each player in turn. For example, "What would you do if you could be any toy for a day—what would you be?" "What would you do if you could be anybody—someone living now or someone from the past—who would you be?" "What would you do if the good fairy came to visit you one night and granted you one wish—what would you wish for?" Hearing everyone's answers will be a lot of fun.

Turn the game around and have everyone answer the question "What would you do if you could change one thing about your life?" You might be surprised at what you hear.

Fabulously Famous Guesses

What famous person would you like to be? Choose one player to start and have him decide on a famous person. The person can be real (even someone from the past), a cartoon character, or a character in a book or movie. The other players, in turn, will ask questions to figure out who that person is, and their questions can only be answered with a yes or no. The person who guesses correctly is the next to select a famous person. Let's say that you have decided to be George Washington. Players might ask:

Are you alive now?	*Answer:* No
Are you a female?	*Answer:* No
Did you have a beard?	*Answer:* No
Were you a pilot?	*Answer:* No
Were you in politics?	*Answer:* Yes
Are you Martin Luther King?	*Answer:* No
Were you a President?	*Answer:* Yes
Are you John Kennedy?	*Answer:* No
Are you George Washington?	*Answer:* Yes!

If you want to set some limits for the game, you might allow a set number of wrong guesses per player or set a time limit.

Catching Categories

Strawberries, apples, bananas, oranges, kiwis. How many items can you name in a category? Select any category, such as fruits, movies, countries, colors, games, TV shows, or any other one that comes to mind. The object of this game is to see how far you can go naming things for the chosen category. Let's say you choose movies as your category. The first player might say *Beauty and the Beast*, the second player, *The Fox and the Hound*, the third player, *Sister Act*, and so on. Once you have exhausted all your ideas for that category, choose a new one and begin another round.

Another way to play is to think up items in a category, and say them to the beat of a clapping, slapping, snapping rhythm. The first player thinks of a category, such as vegetables. All the players begin by clapping their hands twice, then slapping their thighs twice, then snapping their fingers twice. The first player says the word "Category" as everyone is clapping their hands and slapping their thighs, and then "Vegetables," for example, as they are snapping their fingers. The next player adds her item to the category while snapping her fingers.

Player one:	*clap, clap*	
	slap, slap	Say "Category"
	snap, snap	Say "Vegetables"

Player two:	clap, clap	
	slap, slap	
	snap, snap	Say "Peas"
Player three:	clap, clap	
	slap, slap	
	snap, snap	Say "Corn"

A player who cannot come up with an item, gets mixed up, or repeats an item already mentioned is out. The last remaining player chooses the next category.

Secret Vacation

What's your secret vacation? Choose a player to start. That player pretends that he has gone on a vacation or trip somewhere (it can be anywhere in the world), but no one knows where it is. The other players ask questions to figure out where he is vacationing. The player who discovers where it is is the next one to take a secret vacation.

Wheel of Words

Round and round, choose some letters, guess the word. The first player secretly decides on a word and then tells the other players the letter it begins with. The object of this game is for the players to correctly identify the word. Each player begins by asking whether the word includes a letter of his choosing, using each letter as a clue to help determine the word. The winner is the person who figures out the word first. That person then selects the next word.

For example, if the word was "water":

Player one:	"My word starts with W."
Player two:	"Does it have an O?"
Player one:	"No."
Player three:	"Does it have an E?"
Player one:	"Yes."
Player two:	"Does it have an A?"
Player one:	"Yes."
Player three:	"Does it have an R?"
Player one:	"Yes."

Player two:	"Is the word 'wear'?"
Player one:	"No."
Player three:	"Does it have an H?"
Player one:	"No."
Player two:	"Does it have an L?"
Player one:	"No."
Player three:	"Does it have a T?"
Player one:	"Yes."
Player two:	"Is the word 'water'?"
Player one:	"Yes."

A, My Name Is Alice

Who is Alice? Who is her friend? Where does she come from? And what is she selling? Choose a player to start. That player begins with the letter A and says "A, my name is (blank), my friend's name is (blank), we come from (blank) to sell you (blank)," using an A word for each blank. The sentence, for

example, could be "A, my name is Alice, my friend's name is Al, we come from Alabama to sell you apples." The next player would begin with B. For example, "B, my name is Betty, my friend's name is Bill, we come from Buffalo to sell you bananas." If you cannot think of a phrase with your letter on your turn, you are out. The game continues through the letter Z.

You can also play this game in rounds for each letter of the alphabet. On the first round each player would make up the phrase with the letter A. For three players, the round might go like this:

Player one: "A, my name is Ann, my friend's name is Annabelle, we come from Arkansas to sell you artichokes."

Player two: "A, my name is Adam, my friend's name is Arthur, we come from Antarctica to sell you airplanes."

Player three: "A, my name is Allie, my friend's name is Alex, we come from Atlanta to sell you artwork."

Play moves to the letter B after each player has had a chance at making up a phrase with A. As before, if you cannot think of a phrase with your letter on your turn, you are out. The game continues in rounds through the alphabet.

Padiddle

How many broken headlights, turn signals, or brake lights can you spot? You can play this game in one of two ways. In the first, anytime a player spots a broken headlight, turn signal, or brake light, she says "Padiddle." In the second, players try to spell "Padiddle." For each broken headlight, turn signal, or brake light, a letter is given, beginning with P, followed by A, then D, and so on, until one player has spelled the entire word. This game is especially fun at night.

The Minister's Cat

What kind of cat does the minister have? You describe it. Decide who will be first, second, third, depending on how many of you there are.

The first player begins by saying "The minister's cat is a (fill in the blank) cat," using a word to describe the minister's cat that begins with the letter A. For example, "The minister's cat is an adorable cat." The next player comes up with another word describing the minister's cat, for example, "The minister's cat is an awesome cat." Play continues with each player filling in with an A word. If a player cannot think of an A word, he's out. When everyone has had a chance at A, the next player begins with a B word.

If there aren't many players or you want to make the game a bit easier, you might set a limit of three misses before a player is out. You can also make this game a bit more challenging by requiring that all the words you use to describe the minister's cat be silly or whatever other criteria you can all agree on.

Adding On and On and On

Can you complete the alphabet by adding word after word after word? The first player begins a sentence by saying "I know a (fill in the blank)," beginning with the letter A. The second player repeats the first player's phrase and adds a phrase beginning with the letter B. Each player, in turn, repeats the entire phrase and adds on a new phrase using the next letter. The game continues through the entire alphabet.

It might go like this, for example: "I know an alligator." "I know an alligator with a baseball." "I know an alligator with a baseball and a comic book." "I know an alligator with a baseball and a comic book and a doughnut," and so on through the alphabet. If you cannot remember the phrase or add to it with your letter, you are out. The last remaining player wins.

Word Safari

You are on a safari. You're hunting for words. Choose one player to start. That player looks around, finds a word (such as "restaurant," "fuel," or "exit"), and tells everyone what it is. The other players try to find the word again. The player who spots the word first selects the next word to find.

You can also try playing this game using the radio. Turn on the radio. The first player decides on a word. The player who hears the word on the radio first wins, and this player is the next to choose the word to listen for.

Plainy Plates

The map in the back of this book will be fun to look at while playing this game. As you are traveling, look at all the different license plates on the cars you see. To play this game, count the number of different state license plates you see on cars or trucks passing by. The first person to spot five different state plates wins the game. If you reach five in a short period of time, set a higher limit, such as ten. Alaska and Hawaii are hard plates to spot, so if you do see them, give yourself two points instead of one.

Not only do license plates have the state on them, they also have the county, such as Fulton County in Georgia, Fairfield County in Connecticut, Dade County in Florida, or Orange County in California. If you find that you are repeatedly noticing just one state, try seeing how many different counties you can spot within a state. You'll learn a

lot about the state that way. You can play this in two ways. One, have everyone play together and see how many different counties you can find within a set time period, say five minutes. Or have everyone play by themselves and see who can find five different counties first.

That's All, Folks

That's all, folks. It's a wrap. Cut! One player creates her own idea for a movie but keeps the audience in suspense by not finishing it. The other players each make up an ending for the film. Who had the best ending? The funniest? The saddest? The scariest?

License Plate Bingo

Letter bingo. A game of chance in which players find the letters of a chosen word from license plates. Choose one player as the caller. That person will decide on a five- to eight-letter word or phrase, such as pizza, go fish, ice cream, or ninja. The object of this game is to see who can spell the caller's word or phrase first by spotting the letters, in order, on passing license plates from cars, trucks, or buses.

The race is on. You can choose a letter from anywhere on the license plate, but only one person can claim the letter and you can use only one letter per license plate. Play continues until one person has found all the letters in the correct order to spell the caller's word or phrase. When you have completed the word, yell "BINGO!" Now you become the caller.

From 100 to 1

Try your skill! Reverse the usual order of things. The purpose of this game is to count backward from 100 to 1. Choose one player to be the timer. The timer uses the second hand of her watch or the clock or, lacking both of these, counts as the game is going on. Each player starts at 100 and counts backward to 1. Whoever misses a number

is out. Other players listen for mistakes. The timer keeps track of how long it takes each player. The player to count backward from 100 to 1 without any mistakes in the shortest time is the winner.

Practice and see how fast you can count back. How far can each player count back in a minute? In thirty seconds? Who got all the way from 100 to 1?

Conquered the numbers? Try letters. Each player starts at Z and recites the alphabet backward from Z to A. The player who correctly says the alphabet backward from Z to A in the shortest time is the winner. See who can go the farthest in a minute; in thirty seconds.

Rhythmic Rhymes

You are traveling and seeing all sorts of things. Pick any one, then see if you can think of some-thing to rhyme with it. For example, on an airplane you see a seat belt, and you come up with "tuna-melt." Or on the side of the road you see a spotted dog, so you create "potted log." Or walking in front of the White House, you think of "little mouse" to rhyme with White House. Each player takes a turn rhyming.

Counting Continuously

How many numbers in a row can you find using only car license plates? The object of this game is for each player to try to run up a continuous string of numbers taken from car license plates. Set a goal of ten, fifteen, twenty, or twenty-five numbers.

Numbers may appear anywhere on the license plate. Two-digit numbers, such as 15, must appear in the correct order. If you spot a license

plate with AKZ951, for example, you have found your 1. If you need the number 10, you might find it on a license plate with AMD103, one in which the number 10 appears.

Letters also appear on most license plates. Try looking for the letters of the alphabet, beginning with A and going as far as you can. How many in a row can you spot?

People Count

One, two, three, four . . . one hundred. Play this game while you are traveling through a city, waiting in line at the movies, or anywhere you might see a lot of people. Players are restricted to the side of the car they are on or their side of the waiting room or line. Each player starts counting the number of people he sees. (Remember to count on your side only.) The first person to count to 100 wins. Instead of just counting people in general, you might break it down and count boys, girls, babies, blondes, or any other group you can think of.

Another way to play this game is to choose something other than people to count—for example, signs, trees, cows, houses, billboards, tractor trailers, sports cars, or convertibles.

Stare Master

Who can keep a straight face and stare into the eyes of their TravelMate the longest? No blinking, no laughing, no talking. Once you choose a partner, the only skill required in this game is to become the Stare Master. Which one of you can out stare the other?

Feeling a little more animated? Try this version. One TravelMate chooses to be the Stare Master, not blinking an eye, while the other takes whatever steps needed to make her laugh. All facial expressions are allowed and encouraged. Some examples might include: making a fish face by puffing your cheeks in and out, pulling your ear while sticking your tongue out, turning your sun- or eyeglasses upside down, squinting, squirming, shaking, or rolling your eyes while creating musical mouth sounds.

Goofy Golden Rules

Ever feel like making up your own rules? These are goofy golden rules, certainly not what your mom or dad would teach you, but what you might enjoy thinking up and saying. Life could definitely be different. Create your own, go for it, and be goofy. Some ideas to get you started:

If you spill your milk, don't worry—leave it there, the cat will drink it.

If you swallow a coin and it does not come out, do not worry—you have just started your first savings account.

It's not polite to eat with your hands—so try your elbows.

Work together or take turns to develop life's little golden rules.

Twenty Questions

A tried-and-true guessing game. The object of this game is to correctly identify the secret object chosen by the first player, who is "It," in twenty

questions. "It" thinks of an object and tells the other players which category—animal, vegetable, or mineral—contains what she is thinking of. The other players, in turn, will ask questions about the mystery object which can only be answered by yes or no.

Players should ask general questions first and then more specific ones. "It" keeps track of the number of questions that have been asked. If twenty are asked without a guess, "It" tells the other players what the secret object was and remains "It." If another player has correctly guessed the object, he is "It" for the next round of the game.

To help you with the categories, here are some definitions:

Animal Any living thing including animals, people, bugs, etc., and anything made from them, such as leather, wool, milk, cheese, egg, feathers, fur, etc.

Vegetable Any plant, tree, bush, flower, or anything made from them, such as paper, cotton, rubber, string, wood, rope, etc.

Mineral Any solid material not found in nature, such as metal, plastic, glass, stone, oil, pottery, or anything synthetic.

Road Sign Roundup

Have you ever noticed when you are traveling in a car or on a train how many signs there are along the way? These signs warn people about certain things, tell them not to do certain things, or give them instructions in pictures or words or both. In this game, players count the number of different road signs they see. The first player to spot ten different signs wins the game.

To make the game a little more challenging, you might limit the signs to picture signs only or to a specific type of sign—pedestrians crossing, for example.

Buzz

This game will challenge your counting skills and your brain power. The object is to count off continuously substituting the word "Buzz" for the number 5 or any multiple of 5. Choose the order in which you will count off and begin a game like this:

Player one:	"One"
Player two:	"Two"
Player three:	"Three"
Player one:	"Four"
Player two:	"Buzz"

Continue counting but substitute the word "Buzz" for any multiple of 5. For example, 10 would be "Buzz," 15 would be "Buzz," and 20 would be "Buzz." Anyone who does not say "Buzz" when they should is out. Count as fast as you can. The last player left wins.

For a brain teaser, you can try substituting "Buzz" for any two numbers and say "Buzz" for either the numbers or their multiples. For example, if you choose 3 and 7, you would begin 1, 2, "Buzz," 4, 5, "Buzz," "Buzz," 8, "Buzz," 10, 11, "Buzz," 13, "Buzz," "Buzz," 16, 17, "Buzz," 19, 20, "Buzz."

Third and Fourth Grade: Think and Do It for Fun

Galloping Guesses

Put on your guessing hats. There are three places where you can play—in a car, at a restaurant, or in a doctor's office—each with their own variety of play. Choose one person to be the leader. If you are in a car, try to guess (1) the speed the car is traveling at a given time, (2) when the car has traveled a mile, or (3) when a minute has elapsed. If you are the leader and you are playing the first version, look to see what speed the car is traveling and ask the other players to guess it. For the second version, give a signal to start, which tells the other players to try to guess when the car has traveled a mile. In playing the third version, give a signal to start and ask the other players to tell you when they think a minute has elapsed.

At a restaurant, each player will take turns guessing (1) how long it will take before the waiter takes your order, (2) how long it will take before your food arrives, or (3) how much the check will be.

At the doctor's office, take a guess (1) how long it will be before you are called, (2) how long it will be before you actually see the doctor, or (3) how many children will go in before you do.

Sounding the Same

Many words sound the same but have different meanings and spellings. The object of this game is to choose a word, spell it, and challenge your TravelMates to name another word that sounds the same (these are known as homophones). The word should have a different spelling and meaning, such as meet/meat, way/weigh, sum/some, made/maid, or red/read. The next round begins with the second player, and the third with the third player, and so on.

Now that you have really mastered homophones, we have a more difficult version for you. The object of this game is for you to give clues about the two words and see if the other players can guess the homophone. The first player thinks of a homophone—their/there, for example—and might say, "I'm thinking of a homophone, and the first word means place and the second means belonging to them." Whoever guesses there/their would decide on the next homophone and give the definitions.

Alphabet Soup

It's time for some alphabet soup. Choose a subject, such as girls' names, magazines, cars, types of animals (horses, dogs, cats, birds, or wild animals), holidays, TV shows, or any other that appeals to you. The object of this game is to see how far you can go in the alphabet naming as many things possible for each letter of the alphabet for the chosen subject. Player one thinks of something beginning with A, player two thinks of something with B, player three with C, and so

on. For example, the first game might start with girls' names. The first player could say Abby, the next player could say Betsy, the next player could say Chelsea, and so forth. If you cannot think of something with the letter you're up to at your turn, you are out. The game continues through the letter Z. When you have gone through the alphabet, choose another subject and start a new round.

You can also play this game in rounds for each letter of the alphabet. On the first round all players would name something for the subject beginning with A. If anyone cannot think of a word, they would lose their turn. Play moves to the letter B when each player has had a chance at naming something with A. The game continues in rounds through the alphabet.

Math on the Go

Traveling math. Put on your thinking cap and use license plates, road signs, route numbers, or menus to create math problems. Choose one player to start. That person develops a math problem for the other players to solve. For example, she may ask you to add together all the numbers on the license plate of a chosen car; if the license plate is SKY 385, the answer would be 16. Or on a menu, add together the prices for three entrees—$2.95 plus $4.95 plus $4.95 would equal $12.85.

For more advanced play, players might be asked to add together the first two numbers of the license plate and multiply it by the third number. If the license plate was AMJ 484, for example, the answer would be 48. On a menu, you might add together the prices for three entrees (the $12.85)

and then subtract the price of one dessert, say $1.95, so the answer would be $10.90.

You can play this game two ways. Either assign the problem to one player, and when that player has solved it he will develop a problem for the next player, or have everyone solve it. The first to do so correctly will decide on the next problem. You can decide on how hard the problems will be.

Scribble Scrabble

Scribble your name in your head. Now scrabble it. How many words can you make out of your name? The first player starts with his name, say Michael. The object of this game is for each player to take a turn and make up a word with the letters from the name. Michael could become "him," "me," "ham," "he," "hi," "came," "calm." When you cannot think of any more words, switch to another player's name.

For variety, choose a one-word product like cereal. Start with one type, such as Cheerios, and see how many words you can make up with the letters. Cheerios could become "so," "her," "rid," "his," "rose," "rise," "chose." When you've finished scrabbling, try another kind of cereal. Once you've exhausted cereals, move on to another category. Cars, states, colors, and fruits are a few ideas.

Where Am I Going?

Where are you traveling? Choose a player to start. The first player begins with the letter A. The other players ask questions, trying to figure out where she is traveling. With the letter A, you

might decide on Alabama, Argentina, the Amazon, or Atlanta. Questions can only be answered with a yes or no. For example, "Is it cold?" "Is it in Europe?" "Is it in the South?" The player who discovers where the first player is traveling is the one to start with B. Play continues through the letter Z.

You can also play this game by deciding and announcing ahead of time the destination you will be traveling to—for example, Europe or California. Let's say you have chosen Washington, D.C., as the destination (which you have told everyone). The object of the game is to guess the place—the Lincoln Memorial, for example. A third way to play is to have the player to your right give you a letter that the destination has to start with, but not X, Y, or Z. The entire game can also be played with the same letter.

Simply Superlatives

Superlatives are adjectives (words that describe something). When you put the word "most" in front of a word or add an "iest" or "est" to the end of it, it means the best or something that is better than all other things. Some examples of superlatives are hottest, craziest, largest, brightest, most wonderful, most tiring, etc.

Player one thinks of a superlative, such as "funniest," and asks the other players, "Who's the funniest person you know?" Each player answers and then the second player asks a similar question with a different superlative. Everyone is a winner.

This game can also be played by asking a question and having the other players answer it with a superlative. If, for example, you ask,

"What kind of sunset did you see?" Possible answers might be "The most beautiful," "The reddest," or "The brightest."

Jumping Geography

What states border the Mississippi River? How many southern states can you name? How many state capitals can you rattle off? How many states can you name beginning with the letter A? What states were on the Oregon Trail? Play in teams, by yourself, or as a group. If you have trouble or need to check an answer, consult the map in the back of the book.

Silly Phrases on the Move

These silly phrases are made from car license plates. Use the letters from the license plate of a car you have chosen. For example, if the license plate was AKZ 975, you might say, "All kites zoom," or if it was PRP 233, you might say, "Pets read papers." All players can work on the phrases together or you can require each player to develop a phrase of her own.

You can also play this game by creating backward silly phrases, reversing the letters on the license plate. If the license plate that you have chosen was USY 479, for example, you might say "Yams ski uphill," or if it was CMD 399, you might say, "Ducks melt chocolate."

Make Me a Sentence

How many words can you think of beginning with the same letter that will make up a sentence? The object of this game is to make a sentence of four or more words using one letter of the alphabet. Play this game in rounds by having each player make up a sentence made up entirely of words beginning with A, before going on to B, and so on. For example, the first round might go like this:

Player one: "Arthur ate apples alone."   Player two: "Ashley asked Annie anyway."

Player three: "Anthony's aunt admired an animal."

Any player who cannot come up with an appropriate sentence loses his turn.

Feeling competent, you can now try playing where each player helps to create the sentence. The rule is for each player to make the sentence a little longer by adding two words of the same letter. Player one begins with A, player two with B, and so on. Play continues until the sentence cannot go on. If a player cannot continue the sentence, just start a new one, the first two words beginning with A. As these whimsical sentences are created, there are bound to be a lot of laughs. Here's how a game might go:

Player one: Arthur ate   Player two: blueberry bananas

Player three: chewing cautiously   Player one: dribbling delicately

Player two: everywhere evenly

Continue through the alphabet. When you cannot go on, start a new sentence.

Shop Till You Drop

Pretend you are going on a shopping spree. It could be at the grocery store, hardware store, toy store, or department store. The first player begins the game by saying, "I went to the (player chooses type of store) store and bought (fill in the blank)," the item beginning with the letter A. The next player repeats the sentence and adds what he purchased, beginning with the letter B. Each player, in turn, continues through the alphabet. For example, "I went to the grocery store and bought asparagus," says the first player. The second player could say, "I went to the grocery store and bought asparagus and beans," and the third player could say, "I went to the grocery store and bought asparagus and beans and caramels." A player who cannot think of something beginning with his letter, or forgets the shopping list as it has been constructed so far, is out. The last remaining player wins.

You can also play this game in rounds for each letter of the alphabet. For example, beginning with the letter A and going around, each person would repeat the sentence "I went to the grocery store and bought (fill in the blank)," naming something beginning with A, like artichokes, aspirin, or apricots. When someone cannot think of an item beginning with A, she loses her turn in that round. The next player begins with B, naming something like butter, brisket, beets, or bologna. The game continues through the letter Z.

Broadcast News

"Good-evening, this is (name) from WTM News in (city or town). Our lead story tonight concerns (subject)." Choose a TravelMate to be an anchorperson—a person who leads a news broadcast. The news will take place live from any studio location of your choice, such as your hotel room, your car, or a restaurant. Other players become correspondents—people who report on various stories, the weather, sports, or entertainment. The anchorperson begins the news coverage by reporting the main stories of the day, and then turns to the correspondents for other news stories. Each correspondent proceeds to make up her own subject.

A slight twist brings the anchor team to a location outside the studio, such as the Olympic stadium, a baseball field, a farm, or the opening of a movie. A story can be true or total nonsense. Each player is a participant, playing a role in the news event. The correspondent—who you have chosen ahead of time—interviews each player about her role in or opinion relating to the news event.

Play might go like this, "This network news update is coming to you live from the Red Top Farm in Fairbury, Illinois, where Carrie, a nine-year-old, has just shown us her dog who can climb up and down trees." Other story ideas could include: someone who has won the lottery, a blizzard, the sighting of the Lochness Monster in the Potomac River, or a child who has set a record in long distance sprinting.

Word Chameleons

Change a word like a chameleon changes its color. The object of this game is to make a new three- to five-letter word from the previous player's word, starting with the last letter of the word. For example, if player one were to say "sat," player two would have to say a three- to five-letter word beginning with the last letter of "sat," which is T, so she could say "tea." The next player must say a word beginning with A, such as "apple." Players are out when they cannot think of a word.

Or you can go backward, making a new word starting with the middle letter of the previous player's word. For example, if player one said "ten," you could say "end," and the next player could say "not." Use your brain power and have fun.

Double Trouble

Double the fun, double the word. Player one chooses a word that is made up of two words, such as jigsaw. The next player makes a new word by starting with the last part of the first player's word (in this case, saw) and adding another word (horse, for example), thereby creating a new word: sawhorse. Other examples: treetop/tophat, outside/sidewalk, baseball/ballpark. Play in rounds until you run out of words. There's trouble when you cannot double the previous player's word and come up with a new one: You're out!

To play a different way, you might see how many double-trouble words you can think up within a time limit, such as a minute or two. You could also play by going from player to player, with each one saying a compound word, then total how many words everyone named in a minute.

Simply the Same

So many words in the English language mean the same thing. The object of this game is to choose a word and challenge your TravelMates to name a word that has the same meaning, such as "serpent" and "snake," or "happy" and "glad." The next round begins with the second player selecting a new word, the third round begins with the third player, and so on.

You can also play this game by having each player use his word in a sentence. Each player, in turn, would repeat the sentence but use a synonym for the previous player's word. For example:

Player one:	"That's a big piece of chocolate cake."
Player two:	"That's a large piece of chocolate cake."
Player three:	"That's a huge piece of chocolate cake."

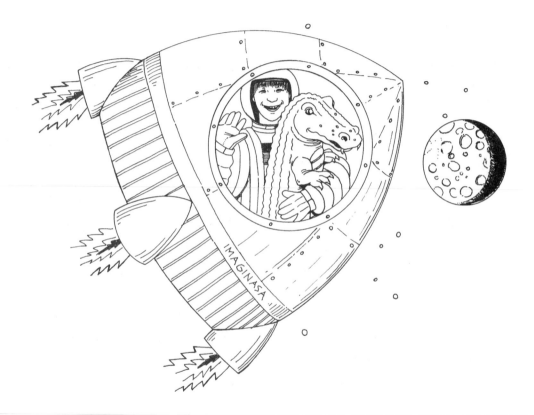

I'm Going to the Moon

I'm going to the moon and I want you to come, but to do so you have to break the code. There are several categories you can choose from, such as spelling your own name, zoo animals, food items, breeds of dogs, or any other one you create. The player chosen to start selects a category but keeps it to herself. For example, the player may choose to spell her name, such as Abigail. She starts by saying, "I'm going to the moon and bringing an alligator." The next player repeats the phrase "I'm going to the moon" and adds something. The trick is for the other players to break the code. To be allowed to come to the moon, each player would have to bring an item that continued the spelling of Abigail. If the chosen item did not continue the spelling of Abigail, they are told they cannot come to the moon on that turn and to try again on the next round. A game might go like this, using Abigail from the name category:

Player one:	"I'm going to the moon and I'm bringing an alligator."
Player two:	"I'm going to the moon and I'm bringing a balloon."
Player one:	"Yes, you can come to the moon."
Player three:	"I'm going to the moon and I'm bringing a cookie."
Player one:	"No, you can't come to the moon. Try again on your next turn."
Player four:	"I'm going to the moon and I'm bringing an icicle."
Player one:	"Yes, you can come to the moon."

Play continues until someone has guessed the code.

For a simpler version, choose a name, and have everyone spell it out in rounds. For example, using the name Maggie:

Player one:	"I'm going to the moon and I'm bringing a mitten."
Player two:	"I'm going to the moon and I'm bringing an apricot."
Player three:	"I'm going to the moon and I'm bringing a gorilla."
Player four:	"I'm going to the moon and I'm bringing a grasshopper."
Player one:	"I'm going to the moon and I'm bringing an igloo."
Player two:	"I'm going to the moon and I'm bringing an egg."

You can continue this game using the names of everyone who is playing.

Silly Shorts

Silly, short phrases can brighten anyone's smile. These silly phrases are only two words long. The first player starts by making up a two-word phrase. The next player makes up a two-word phrase with the first word starting with the first letter of the second word of the previous player's phrase.

For example, if you are first, you say, "Dogs drool." The next player might say, "Dishes float," the next player, "Frogs dance," and so on. If you cannot come up with a new phrase beginning with the first letter of the previous player's second word within an agreed-upon amount of time, you are out. The last player left wins.

Feeling up for a challenge? Try playing this game by making up the two-word phrases with the first word starting with the first two letters of the second word of the previous player's phrase. For example, if you had said, "Dogs bark," the next player might say, "Balls bounce," the next player, "Boats burp," and so on.

Pig Latin

Turn your conversations into pig Latin using this code. See how long you can talk using pig Latin. Here's how it works. Form words by moving the first letter or two (depending on the word) to the end of the word and adding the "ay" sound. For example, "My trip this summer" would become "Ymay iptray isthay ummersay." When the word starts with a vowel, just add "ay" to the end of the word. "Our camera took outrageous pictures," then, would become "Ouray ameracay ooktay outrageousay icturespay."

For a change, try "igpoy atinloy." Instead of the "ay" sound, use the "oy" sound. "I am having fun today. Are you?" would then be "Ioy amoy avinghoy unfoy odaytoy. Areoy ouyoy?"

Let the coded conversation begin!

Spelled the Same

Many words sound the same and are spelled the same but have different meanings. These words are called homonyms. The object of this game is to see how many homonyms each player can come up with during an agreed-upon time limit. To start you thinking, here are some examples: tie—something a man wears and what it is called if a game's score is even; mine—something that belongs to me and a place where you dig for precious metals; plate—something you eat off and what a baseball player crosses to score a run; state—a place you live and how you feel.

You can also play this game by giving clues for the homonyms and having the other players guess what word it is. For example, you might say, "I have a word that means you have done it

correctly and it is a direction. What is my word?" The first player to say "right" is the winner.

Coolest Cars

What car is the coolest? Have each player name what he thinks is the coolest car—for example, Porsche 911, Mercedes 500SL, Mazda MX-5 Miata, Jaguar XJ6, Saab 900, Acura Integra, Chevrolet Corvette, or Pontiac Firebird. The first player to spot his coolest car wins. Let's say that you have chosen a Jeep Cherokee. If one passes you by and you say, "Cool car, a Jeep Cherokee," you are the winner of that round.

You can vary this game by getting players to specify the color the car would have to be. To make it a little harder the winner would have to spot five of his coolest cars. Or you can all play together and select one type of car, such as convertibles, and see how many you can spot in five minutes.

Fifth and Sixth Grade: Challenge Me Now

Ghostbusters

Be a ghostbuster. Make your TravelMates disappear. The object of this game is to create a word by adding letters, without being the one who ends the word. The first player names a letter that begins a word. The second player adds a letter. The player who completes a word receives the letter G from the word "ghost." If you end another word, you take an H. When a player has completed enough words (five) to spell "ghost," he's out. Three-letter words do not count. Players must always have a word in mind when they add a letter or they can be challenged. If you are challenged and you did in fact have a real word in mind, the person who challenged you receives a letter from "ghost." If you did not have a real word in mind, you receive a letter from "ghost."

Here's how a game might go:

First player says:	"R" (thinking of the word rabbit)
Second player says:	"O" (thinking of the word robin)
Third player says:	"A" (thinking of the word road)
First player says:	"R" (which ends the round, spelling the word roar, so he takes the letter G)

You can make this game a little harder by adding letters when you think the word is ended. For example, let's say the word that has been spelled is "travel." It would appear that the word has ended and the person who added the L would receive a letter from "ghost." However, in this version he would announce that the word is not finished. He must have a word in mind—like "TravelMates." The next player would try to build the word further. If she is unable to add another letter, she may challenge him, requiring him to reveal his word. If challenged and unable to add a letter to the word, he receives a letter from "ghost."

What's My Age?

What's my age? Learn a sure way to guess anyone's age every time! Have each player do the following steps silently and then tell you the answer to the last step. With our help you'll get it right every time.

	Examples		
Ask each player to think of his age silently	7	9	12
Tell them to multiply it by three	21	27	36
Add one to the answer	22	28	37
Multiply this number by three	66	84	111
Add their age to the answer, and say the number out loud	73	93	123

The answer will always be the first digit of this final number. Take 93, for example. Cross off the last digit, the 3. When you do that, you get 9. So you know that player is nine years old. Have fun guessing!

Ovenglovish

This game will work your mind and tongue. Turn your conversation in English into a new language called Ovenglovish. Here's how it works. Put an "ov" (pronounced *aaav*) before every sounding vowel in a word. Thus, English becomes Ovenglovish. Another example would be, "I went to the store to buy some milk," which in Ovenglovish would be "Ovi wovent tovo thove stovore tovo bovuy sovome movilk." "I like to travel and play games" becomes "Ovi lovike tovo trovavovel ovand plovay govames."

The basic rules are to make long sounds out of short sounds and to remember that you sometimes have to adapt it in order to pronounce it. While Ovenglovish takes a while to learn, it can provide hours of fun and many laughs.

Feeling confident? You can create another new language, using "av" or "em" instead of "ov." Now you're playing Avenglavish or Emenglemish.

Ridiculously Reversed

You say "der," I say "red." You say "teews," I say "sweet." You say "pleh," I say "help." These ridiculously reversed words will amuse even the most seasoned speller. The first player thinks of a word and spells it backward—"yas" for "say" or "gur" for "rug," for example. Start with short words and increase the length of the words as everyone becomes more comfortable with the game. The first player to correctly say what the word is wins and is the next to go.

Fact, Famous, Fiction

How many famous people can you think of? These people can be historical figures, present-day celebrities, or fictional characters from a book, movie, or cartoon. Choose one player to start. That person begins by saying the first and last name of a famous person. The next player must name a person whose first name starts with the first letter of the last name of the famous person just mentioned.

For example, if the first player says Betsy Ross, the next person could say Rosie O'Donnell, the next person could say Oprah Winfrey, and so on. If you cannot come up with a new person beginning with the letter given within an agreed-upon time limit, you are out. The last player left wins.

To make the game a little more challenging, try naming a person whose first name starts with the second letter of the last name of the famous person previously mentioned. For example, if you are first and say Chelsea Clinton, the next person could say Lois Lane, the next person could say Ace Ventura, and the next person could say Elizabeth Montgomery.

Walloping Why?

Did you ever wonder why the sun rises in the East and sets in the West? Or why the British drive on the left-hand side of the road and the Americans on the right-hand side? There are so many facts that we take for granted. The object of this game is to ask a walloping-why question and have your TravelMates offer their answers. You might not be able to answer the question, but you'll have a lot of laughs listening to everybody's creative reasoning.

Players might ask questions like these:

Why do you get a picture when you turn on the TV set?

Why do yellow and green make blue?

Why do your fingernails grow?

Why is grass green?

Why is the ocean salty?

Why do planets stay in position when there is no gravity in space?

Math Magic

This is almost magic. . . . The object of this game is to correctly guess the number the other player has chosen. Do all the steps silently unless you are asked to say a number out loud. With our help you'll do it right every time.

What's the Number? Multiply, Add, and Divide

	Examples		
Ask each player to think of a number (under 100)	4	5	7
Tell them to multiply it by three	12	15	21
Add six to the answer	18	21	27
Divide it by three, and tell you the answer	6	7	9

The answer will always be two less than the final answer. For example, if the final answer is 7, then the number the player has chosen is 7 minus 2 = 5.

Add It Up, Take It Out

Test your math skills. The object of this game is to bring a sum of numbers to 50 or 100 exactly. The first player chooses a number from 1 to 9. The next player chooses a number from 1 to 9 and adds it to the

first player's number. Each player, in turn, adds a number from 1 to 9 to the previous player's sum, trying to bring the total up to 50 or 100 exactly. To win you must be the one whose addition of a number brings the total to 50 or 100 exactly. The player who does this gets to begin the next round. For example:

Player one:	"I choose 6."
Player two:	"9, 9 plus 6 equals 15."
Player three:	"7, 7 plus 15 equals 22."
Player one:	"8, 8 plus 22 equals 30."
Player two:	"5, 5 plus 30 equals 35."
Player three:	"6, 6 plus 35 equals 41."
Player one:	"9, 9 plus 41 equals 50. I win, my new number is 3."

You can also play this game by choosing any other number for the total, such as 20 or 30. Or for a twist, play by subtracting the number. Begin by choosing a number for the total, such as 50. Then each player, in turn, will choose a number from 1 to 9 and subtract it from the previous player's total until zero is reached. The one who reaches zero first wins.

Here's another twist. In both games, don't get caught reaching the total or zero. If you do, it's a point against you. If you reach five points, you are out. The last remaining player wins.

Geography

This game will challenge your geography skills. The first player names a continent, country, state, city, ocean, river, or lake. The second player must take the last letter of the place named and think of another place that begins with that letter. Places can only be cited once.

For example, the first player might say Nigeria. The next player could say Arkansas, the next player could say Stamford, and so on. If a player cannot come up with a new place beginning with the last letter of the previously mentioned place within an agreed-upon time limit, he's out. The last remaining player wins.

You can try varying this game by limiting it to a certain category—for example, cities or countries only.

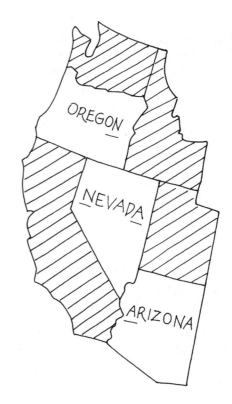

Initially Sports

Michael Jordan, David Justice, Nancy Kerrigan, Babe Ruth, Deion Sanders, Cal Ripken, Andre Agassi—sports greats, easily recognizable until you use their initials. The object of this game is to have one player think of a notable sports figure, say his initials, and challenge his TravelMates to guess who it is. Players should start by asking what sport the person plays. A game might go like this:

Player one:	I've got my person in mind, and his initials are M.J.(Magic Johnson).
Player two:	Does this person play baseball?
Player one:	No.
Player three:	Does this person play basketball?
Player one:	Yes.
Player two:	Is it Michael Jordan?
Player one:	No.
Player three:	Is it Magic Johnson?
Player one:	Yes. It's your turn now.

Purely Politics

Do you know the names of your two Senators? Or the name of the wife of the Vice President? How about the Congressman from your district? Or the Mayor of your city? This game will challenge your knowledge of who's who in public office. One player begins by asking a question, such as "Who is the Governor of Georgia?" In turn, everyone takes a guess until the correct name is mentioned. In this example, the player who says Zell Miller wins and gets to ask the next question.

To broaden the scope of the game, include politicians' relatives in your questions, such as "What is the name of the President's daughter?" Or former elected officials, like past Presidents—for example, "Name all the living former Presidents." For older players, asking them to name their local representatives is another twist.

Figure Me Out

It's a mystery, can you figure it out? The first player thinks of a number between 1 and 500. Each player, in turn, tries to guess the number by asking one question. The player who correctly guesses the number is the next to pick a number. Our hint is to start by always choosing the halfway point of the lowest and highest numbers used and asking if it is greater (or less) than the midpoint number.

For a twist, you win if you *don't* guess the number. The object of this version is to stay away from the number. If you guess the number you are out. The person to your right then selects the next number for everyone "not" to guess. The more players, the better—for both games.

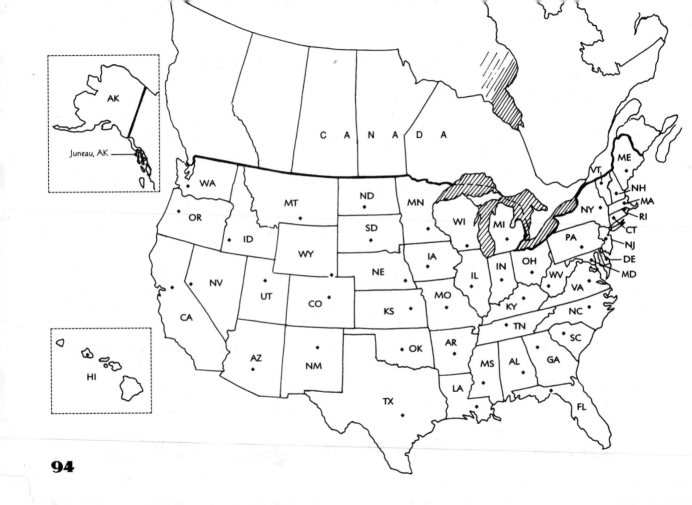

AK

Juneau, AK

HI

WA

OR

ID

MT

ND

MN

SD

WY

NE

IA

WI

MI

CANADA

NV

UT

CO

KS

MO

IL

IN

OH

NY

VT

ME

NH

MA

RI

CT

NJ

DE

MD

PA

WV

VA

KY

TN

NC

SC

CA

AZ

NM

OK

AR

MS

AL

GA

LA

TX

FL

94

The Fifty States and Their Capitals

AL	Alabama ◆ Montgomery	LA	Louisiana ◆ Baton Rouge	OH	Ohio ◆ Columbus
AK	Alaska ◆ Juneau	ME	Maine ◆ Augusta	OK	Oklahoma ◆ Oklahoma City
AZ	Arizona ◆ Phoenix	MD	Maryland ◆ Annapolis	OR	Oregon ◆ Salem
AR	Arkansas ◆ Little Rock	MA	Massachusetts ◆ Boston	PA	Pennsylvania ◆ Harrisburg
CA	California ◆ Sacramento	MI	Michigan ◆ Lansing	RI	Rhode Island ◆ Providence
CO	Colorado ◆ Denver	MN	Minnesota ◆ St. Paul	SC	South Carolina ◆ Columbia
CT	Connecticut ◆ Hartford	MS	Mississippi ◆ Jackson	SD	South Dakota ◆ Pierre
DE	Delaware ◆ Dover	MO	Missouri ◆ Jefferson City	TN	Tennessee ◆ Nashville
FL	Florida ◆ Tallahassee	MT	Montana ◆ Helena	TX	Texas ◆ Austin
GA	Georgia ◆ Atlanta	NE	Nebraska ◆ Lincoln	UT	Utah ◆ Salt Lake City
HI	Hawaii ◆ Honolulu	NV	Nevada ◆ Carson City	VT	Vermont ◆ Montpelier
ID	Idaho ◆ Boise	NH	New Hampshire ◆ Concord	VA	Virginia ◆ Richmond
IL	Illinois ◆ Springfield	NJ	New Jersey ◆ Trenton	WA	Washington ◆ Olympia
IN	Indiana ◆ Indianapolis	NM	New Mexico ◆ Santa Fe	WV	West Virginia ◆ Charleston
IA	Iowa ◆ Des Moines	NY	New York ◆ Albany	WI	Wisconsin ◆ Madison
KS	Kansas ◆ Topeka	NC	North Carolina ◆ Raleigh	WY	Wyoming ◆ Cheyenne
KY	Kentucky ◆ Frankfort	ND	North Dakota ◆ Bismarck